Birding is a rare endeavor that is almost unequaled in its scope. This charming little book touches upon many of the aspects of birding that motivates us (birders). Written from the perspective of a long time birder living in California, stories specific to his life and location illustrate larger, more universal concepts. Beginner birders or people with an interest in learning about birding may discover some new ways of looking at the birding lifestyle. Long-time birders may reawaken their long-forgotten passions about birding as well."

— John Sterling, *Professional Ornithologist*

Why We Bird

DAVID C. RICE

ILLUSTRATIONS BY ROBIN G. PULICH

PUBLISHED BY GOLDEN GATE AUDUBON SOCIETY

Library of Congress Cataloguing-in-Publication Data Available.

ISBN: 978-0-9899767-0-1

Designed by Ellis Myers

Printed by CreateSpace

Published in 2013 by Golden Gate Audubon Society
2530 San Pablo Avenue, Suite G
Berkeley, CA 94702

www.goldengateaudubonsociety.org

www.whywebird.com

For Carol

You always say, whenever I go birding,

"I hope you find your bird."

Contents

Preface

With the increasing popularity of birding over the past fifty years came a new literary genre that explored the experience of looking for birds, looking at birds, and enjoying birds. Let's call them birding books instead of bird books. In the bibliography I list more than twenty of them, most published since 1990. It was not always so. A century ago bird-naturalists sometimes included their own thoughts and feelings, but for the most part they wrote as reporters about the birds themselves. Then came field guides, only about birds. Through it all, nature-writers have included birds in their reflections on the natural world, but usually as part of a more embracing commentary.

Why We Bird began after I read a book that aimed to explain the attractions of birding but missed a lot of what attracted me. Reflecting on forty years of field experiences, I identified my seven core reasons: witnessing their flight, hearing their song, and noticing their color; solving identification challenges; playing Big Day, listing, and chasing games; having an unexpected bird surprise me; joining in efforts to conserve them; coming home with bird stories to tell; and finding solace in them. I hope *Why We Bird* describes some of the reasons you bird ... or will want to.

Introduction

A Western Tanager introduced me to birding. On the other side of a Sierra Nevada creek the yellow bird with a red head and black wings lit up a small pine tree. I wanted a better view but the bird flew away. When I got home I bought my first pair of binoculars and a bird book and identified birds in the local park—goldfinches were really yellow. Soon I began to take short trips to look for birds—was that an eagle?—and then longer trips. Then I signed up for a bird identification class. Why did I want to bird?

After following birds up and down California for most of my adult life, I now agree that, beyond the obvious reasons—"the thrill of the chase, days of companionship outdoors, enigmatic identifications solved, competitions and even score-keeping, witnessing nature in action, times and places of great beauty,"[1]—birding is also "a religious experience,"[2] a way to "feel a kind of belonging,"[3] an "attraction through the spirit,"[4] and "a state of heart ... akin to love ... [for] those extraordinary moments when ... 'life touches life'."[5]

To resurrect an old word, aren't we all ornithophilists—bird lovers, each in our own way?

1. Todd Newberry, *The Ardent Birder* (Berkeley, CA, Ten Speed Press, 2005) 4.

2. Leonard Nathan, *Diary of a Left-Handed Birdwatcher* (San Diego, CA, Harcourt Brace and Co., 1996) 118.

3. Jeremy Mynott, *Birdscapes* (Princeton, NJ, Princeton University Press, 2009) 302.

4. John Hay, *The Great House of Birds* (San Francisco, CA, Sierra Club Books, 1996) xii.

5. Newberry, 4.

Birds begin and end beyond us, out of reach and outside our thought, and we see them doing things apparently without feeling or thinking, but—and because of this—they make us think and feel.

 Tim Dee

Flight, Song, Color

Birds bewitch us. We try to see or hear them, are happy when we do, and think about them when we don't. A bird flies above us. If we could fly, we might leave our troubles behind and escape to wherever we wanted, whenever we wanted. We watch and wish. Gravity has us on a short leash.

Tule Lake, near the California–Oregon border, is one of the Klamath Basin National Wildlife Refuges, where hundreds of Bald Eagles winter along with over a million ducks, geese, and swans. One January I brought four friends, whom I called the hawk-guys because they liked big birds best, to see a spectacle they had never seen before.

We started at the refuge's visitor center early in the morning and drove the auto loop from west to east. Everyone wanted to see the eagles, but we saw waterfowl first. Swans took off; their long necks seemed to pull them forward. When they landed, the loud splash sounded like an accident. Ducks dashed by and gave us only a brief glimpse of color or shape before they were gone. The geese flew slowly enough to let us inspect them.

We got out of the van. If we had worn feathers we would not have needed our jackets, sweaters, hats, and gloves to protect us from the cold wind. Lines of Snow Geese flew in different directions and at different heights. When they called, the sky echoed. The gray of the clouds intensified their white and black pattern. Had I ever seen birds this clearly?

I knew that in the past the Klamath Basin held, not one million, but six million waterfowl in winter. Still, I thought the world had never been as full of geese, ducks, and swans as it was that day: flying through the air, floating on the water, feeding in the fields. The hawk-guys were impressed. They had never seen so many big birds at one time.

We approached an adult Bald Eagle on a telephone pole. When we got too close it stretched its wings, glided three poles away, and landed. Another one flew across the partially frozen water. I followed it with my binoculars until it reached the far shore. Its white head, black body, and white tail were still easily visible. We all watched still another fly from one telephone pole to another. A Bald Eagle in flight always commands attention.

After the road left the water's edge, Red-tailed Hawks circled lazily above us, and Northern Harriers unhurriedly scoured each inch of each ditch. A Short-eared Owl perched on a bush and then whispered away to a more distant bush. Were we near a subterranean mouse factory?

We drove the auto loop again—this time from east to west—in the late afternoon. Most of the waterfowl had settled down for the night; hundreds of Snow Geese were floating together in large white drifts. At dusk, back near the visitor center, we saw one, two, five, ten Great Horned Owls perched on the telephone poles along the road. As we passed one owl after another, after another, I was tempted to trade in my DNA for an owl model. Flying in the dark would be a double wonder.

Once the hawk-guys and I waited in the foothills for a Barn Owl to leave its day roost. The harriers disappeared with the light. Then we glimpsed the owl flying toward us along a fence line. It came closer, closer, closer. It swerved and crossed the road. We were five feet away, face-to-face with a Barn Owl before it veered. Rick Wright said "discovery is great fun, but being discovered touches us more deeply" and called moments like this "not just gratuitous but grace-ridden, less accomplishment than gift."[1]

If birds were like butterflies, visually compelling but silent, we would still watch them, but sight is superfluous when a bird is singing and your ears overflow with song. The Pacific (aka Winter) Wren's effervescent riff never fails to amaze and the Hermit Thrush's hymn through a mountain forest has brought tears. If you listen to birds, you probably have your own favorites.

Swainson's Thrush is one of my top ten. Its song is blossoms rising into pink dawn or purple twilight. One June I car-camped with my wife, Carol, in the coastal redwoods of northwestern California. The first evening, as Swainson's Thrush songs floated through the forest, she said, "That's my favorite birdsong." It took longer than usual to finish our breakfast the next morning; when we chewed, we could not hear the thrushes well, so we paused longer between mouthfuls.

Sandhill Cranes sound more like drummers than singers, but they also rank near the top of my list. One March day Carol and I drove down a country road south of Sacramento to look for them. The fields had not yet been re-planted, and when we arrived a few cranes were feeding on last year's leftovers. Some were already leaping and flapping in their courtship dance. They would soon leave for their breeding grounds farther north.

We could see trucks silently traveling up and down Interstate 5, a few miles away. The cacophony of vehicles, airplanes, radios, and power tools that frequently drowns out birdsong has made listening to birds harder than it used to be, but on this early spring afternoon our ears had the cranes to themselves.

---

1. Rick Wright, "Discovery" (*Winging It*, American Birding Association, 2006) 2.

The cranes on the ground called intermittently. When small flocks flew in, the birds called continuously until they landed. I saw their beaks open and close, and an instant later heard their percussive voices. That pause between the sight of the crane's beak opening and closing and the sound reaching my ears was like the pause between a storm's lightning and thunder, and it made the cranes' calls both familiar and ominous.

Snow Goose

As dusk approached, the soundscape changed. Hundreds of crows cawed their way west toward their night roost, and small flocks of noisy White-fronted Geese landed near us. More and more cranes kept arriving from distant fields. Loud chattering announced a large flock of Snow Geese. With the light almost gone, the chorus of geese and cranes grew louder. "Close your eyes and listen," Carol said. The sound was almost palpable.

Years before, I had waited with the hawk-guys for cranes on one of the few hills in the Carrizo Plain, a mostly uninhabited grassland one hundred miles northwest of Los Angeles. A ranger had told us the cranes would fly in at dusk. It was almost dark before we heard one, and we could not see it. Then the flock appeared, silhouetted against the last light, bugling the day to a close. When they had quieted, I clapped for an encore. Back home, I tried to imitate those cranes for Carol. She laughed then at my guttural incoherence. Now she was a witness.

Sandhill Cranes do not sound like other birds, but what do they sound like? Are they "a pandemonium of trumpets, rattles, croaks, and cries"[1]; "a mellow, penetrating, powerful note, which seems to hawk from the elder Eocene"[2]; or "clarion calls out of the farthest skies, summon[ing] our attention to our own swift passage on this precious earth?"[3] Maybe we use so many images to describe their sounds because we are also trying to describe how those sounds affect us.

Or maybe calling cranes are the soundscape of the sublime, the acoustic equivalent of high mountains. Maybe we feel a sense of awe when we hear them, as we do when we stare at a distant peak or the night sky. No wonder we often talk about the sounds cranes make. Cranes can make us feel insignificant and we want company, or can make us feel so inspired we can't keep quiet.

When a bird is silent, we stare. A breeding warbler's plumage could be the work of some color-crazed wizard. A Black Oystercatcher's bill is candy-cane red, its legs pink, and its red-rimmed eye yellow. How can we not stare?

One clear, warm January day in Northern California some friends and I birded the Crescent City harbor as the tide surged in. An Ancient Murrelet surprised us as it dove and surfaced about thirty yards away. It must have followed the fish in with the tide, since it usually feeds well beyond the surf line. With the light behind us, and the morning sun low in the winter sky, the bird—black, white, and gray with a yellow bill—looked impeccably feathered and lit from within.

Earlier we had stood on a bluff overlooking the ocean and watched a pair of Red-breasted Mergansers feeding. The

1. Aldo Leopold, *A Sand County Almanac* (New York, Ballantine Books, 1974) 101.

2. William Leon Dawson, *The Birds of California, Vol. 3* (San Diego, CA, South Moulton Co. , 1923) 1528.

3. Peter Matthiessen, *The Birds of Heaven: Travels with Cranes* (New York, North Point Press, 2001) 4.

male's green head contrasted sharply with its white neck and bronze-patterned breast band; the female's rusty head brightened her gray body. They dove so frequently it was hard to study them but when I returned home, a painting by Louis Agassiz Fuertes of two male Red-breasted Mergansers showed me what I could not see that morning. One of his birds is in profile and its eye stares penetratingly at the viewer. The other bird faces the viewer and its beak is open. The orange-red gape makes it look ferocious, and would have made me tremble if I were a fish. Yet I still preferred those live mergansers. We were both being lit by the same light.

We also saw two young Harlequin Ducks. After a brief look we moved on. If they had been adult males in their colorful breeding plumage we would have looked longer, but birders rarely watch individual birds for long, no matter how beautiful the birds might be. A bird in view is not worth two still hidden in the bush—and those two, once glimpsed, soon lose their allure, as well, for many of us. It can be a costly trade-off. If we kept looking, we might see something we had never noticed before about that species.

At mid-day we ate our lunch at the public boat ramp beside a large coastal lagoon just north of Crescent City. There were small flocks of ducks on the water—Canvasback, scaup, wigeon. The lagoon used to overflow with ducks in winter. William Brewer wrote about this same area in 1863, "Myriads of ducks and geese and other waterfowl swarmed, and some white swans and pelicans enlightened the scene. These waterfowl, especially ducks, are very abundant. I saw a hunter, an Indian, coming in town with a horse loaded with them. He must have had a hundred."[1] We saw a hunter drive up in his truck and drop a Redhead near his ten-year-old son, who was sitting by the shore. When I looked at the limp bird through

---

1. William H. Brewer, *Up and Down California in 1860-1864* (Berkeley, CA, University of California Press, 1974) 495.

my binoculars from across the parking lot, it did not look luminescent. It must have lost its light when it fell from the sky.

We drove around the lagoon. Small rafts of scaup and wigeon floated on the water, none near shore. Were they trying to stay away from the hunters? We found a large raft of coots swimming so closely together it was difficult to estimate their number. One of my friends found a male Redhead in the middle of the coots. The hunters were not shooting coots. Was the Redhead swimming there to avoid the hunters? Can a bird deliberately dim its light? If I had been that bird, I would have done that.

Sandhill Crane

Another important bit of advice is to view mistakes as an opportunity for learning. Ask yourself why the mistake occurred.

 David Sibley

Identifications

Birders love to identify birds. The shape of the bill, the placement of the eyes, the length of the legs and wings, the color and pattern of the feathers, and the vocalizations all combine to tell us a lot about a bird's way of life. We can determine what species it is and, sometimes, what sub-species. The superb ornithologist Luis Felipe Baptista distinguished song variations in nine different populations of the White-crowned Sparrow in the San Francisco Bay Area. The only limit to identifying birds precisely is the amount of detail we can learn about them. It is even possible to recognize some of them as individuals which, of course, they do with each other.

One July my birding friend Helen and I studied southwardly migrating shorebirds at some sewage ponds in the Central Valley. Aside from the wildlife refuges, these ponds are the only "shore" in the inland sea of agricultural fields and subdivisions. Not as daunting as gulls, yet complex enough to challenge anyone, shorebirds are accessible, colorful, and highly variable: the more you look, the more you see.

At the birder-friendly Madera Sewage Ponds we found a mixed shorebird flock feeding at the muddy edge of a shallow pond. It was hot. We did not mind. The dowitchers' breasts were shades of burgundy, the sandpipers' backs were shades of brown and rufous, and the yellowlegs' legs were fresh-paint yellow. There were no rare shorebirds, but Killdeer, avocets, and stilts added oranges, reds, and black-and-whites to the bird color wheel.

The sandpipers flushed. Shorebird flocks are easy to love. First there are fifty (or a hundred, or two hundred) birds feeding on a mudflat. Then they take off and meld into a flock that rises, turns, and turns again in unison, suggesting all the birds are connected to each other. Then the flock lands on the mudflat and, simultaneously, the birds return to their separate identities. I never tire of seeing this transformation. If the light is right and the birds distant enough, the whole flock can disappear from view when it turns. When it turns again it re-appears, as if by magic.

When my wife and I camped for a week at Mono Hot Springs in the southern Sierra, I walked along the south fork of the San Joaquin River. A little dark gray rock in the middle of the stream flew away. Another one splashed onto a log and blinked. Dipper. An easy bird to identify but, after naming it, I kept looking. A dipper makes a mountain stream even more playful. It bobs like an aquatic gym instructor. There, the rock moved. The dipping dipper dipped again. I was tempted to play follow-the-leader with that dipper, walk up and down the stream with it, bob when it bobbed, blink when it blinked.

One morning I studied the plumage of an Empidonax flycatcher—was it a Willow or a Dusky? One morning I happily memorized the contact call of the Mountain Quail; so that's what that sound is. Elliott Coues said, "… I have never yet walked in the woods without learning something pleasant that I did not know before … How then can you, with so much before you, keep out of the woods another minute?"[1]

On the way home we stopped at the ranger station. Pictures of Sierra Nevada birds hung from the walls. Two men in their twenties came in, looked at the Clark's Nutcracker, and agreed that was the bird they had seen near their camp. I hoped they would learn the names of more mountain birds someday.

1. Elliott Coues, *Key to North American Birds, Vol 1* (New York, Arno Press, 1974) 11.

American Dipper

Bird identification is part problem-solving and part sheer satisfaction at knowing the solution. But seeing a bird well does not ensure we will name it correctly. As David Sibley reminds us, "The fact that the living bird is a shy and wary creature, with no particular interest in being seen, means that the challenge of matching the details of the bird's appearance to a picture is compounded by the challenge of seeing and interpreting the details in the first place."[2] Still, experienced birders identify most birds accurately.

But not always. My most memorable misidentification occurred one fall day in 1994. I was birding with three friends on the Central California coast south of Morro Bay. Around noon we met another birder, who told us there was a Painted Bunting in a nearby town. Painted Bunting is an extremely rare bird in California. We decided to change our plans for the afternoon and go for the bunting.

---

2. David Allen Sibley, *Sibley's Birding Basics* (New York, Alfred A. Knopf, 2002) 3.

15

No other birders were there when we arrived. The man had told us to look for the bird in the first hundred yards of the eucalyptus trees that lined the narrow creek. At first all we saw were Yellow-rumped Warblers. Then we spotted—umm—an American Redstart, an eastern warbler that regularly wanders in the fall to California. We watched it flit from branch to branch for a minute or so, lost it in the foliage, and never saw the Painted Bunting, though we looked for over an hour. The next morning Helen called. She asked me to get out my field guide and look at the picture of the Painted Redstart. When I did, I realized we had seen a Painted Redstart, not an American Redstart.

How did four experienced birders mistake a Painted Redstart for an American Redstart? Because we were looking for a Painted Bunting, because a Painted Redstart is also a California mega-rarity, and because we all knew the probability of a Painted Bunting and a Painted Redstart being in the same place in California at the same time was zero. If beginning birders, struggling with an identification, sometimes look too closely at extraneous field marks, experienced birders sometimes do not look closely enough, because they know too well what birds to expect, and expecting is half of seeing.

In retrospect we should have questioned why we were looking for a Painted Bunting in a eucalyptus tree; Painted Buntings are seed eaters. Our informant obviously meant to say "Painted Redstart." What went wrong? I think the answer lay in, or rather on, the National Geographic Field Guide he was holding when he spoke to us. There are five birds on that guide's cover; one of them is a Painted Bunting. I bet that painted picture of the bunting led to his slip. All five of us goofed.

All birders misidentify birds. If a friend corrects us before we realize our mistake, we may feel chagrined. If we miscall a bird in front of birders we do not know well, or who are more experienced than we are, we may feel embarrassed and fear our reputation as a birder has at least wobbled. To ease the discomfort of birder error, my friends and I have adopted the "you're only as good as your last call" rule. When we mis-identify a bird we quickly look for another one to identify correctly. Mallard! Turkey Vulture! Mourning Dove! Then we can rejoin the knowledgeable birder's club.

We also take a silent vow to look more closely before calling out the next perplexing bird.

Listing is a great game, maybe the greatest. For some, it becomes an obsession that drives all conscious thought and action. (Perhaps a "listers anonymous" group would save a few marriages and friendships.) For some it is a fanciful game of fill-in-the-blanks. For some it becomes a blueprint for scientific investigation.

         ❧ Rich Stallcup

Games

When Pete Dunne asked Roger Tory Peterson "Where is birding going?", he answered "It can be a science, an art, a sport, a game, an ethic, a challenge ..." and, when pressed to elaborate said, "Birding is going EVERYWHERE! Everywhere."[1] Yes. After a forty-year affair with birds, I am still infatuated.

Isn't a Big Day a sporting event? How many different species can we see or hear from midnight to midnight? The sun is the clock. Tomorrow's birds do not count. On the chosen day, we are like some large insect that lives as an adult for only twenty-four hours. Strategy matters as much as birding skills. We have to plan the route, decide how long to stay at each stop, and not get too far behind our schedule. We have to know each bird's habitat; if we do not find the bird there, it may well go unchecked on our Big Day list. Every species matters. Until we have found one, a House Finch is as valuable as a Northern Goshawk. When we find an unexpected bird we are elated. When we miss an expected one we are deflated.

And we all have to try for every bird because one of the American Birding Association's (ABA's) official Big Day rules is that 95% of the day's species have to be seen or heard by all participants in order to "count." At the end of the day, exhausted and perhaps hallucinating the birds we missed, we already start planning for the next Big Day. Athletes always want to break their personal records. Kenn Kaufman describes the experience of doing a Big Day as "... that heightened awareness of the distant and the hidden, that straining for faint sounds

---

1. Pete Dunne, *The Feather Quest: A North American Birder's Year* (New York, Dutton, 1992) 314, 316.

and subtle movements, while shutting out anything that is not a potential New Bird ... in which views of birds are measured in milliseconds, in which bird songs are classified instantly and then ignored, in which no precious moment of daylight could be wasted on aesthetics."[1]

One year Helen and I did a Big Day in late September in Nevada County, which stretches from the foothills to the mountains in north-central California. We were competing in the San Francisco Bay Bird Observatory's Fall Challenge. The team that found the most birds in any California county would win a spotting scope, and so would the team that found the highest percentage of regularly occurring birds in any California county.

We arrived after dark at a hunter's campground and decided to get up at first light. Hard-core birders start at midnight but we were not going to win a scope. Big Days involve birding by ear as much as possible; in many places it is easier to hear birds than see them. We had not done enough ear-training to win a prize.

I fell asleep and woke with a dream of a Glaucous Gull. I fell back to sleep and dreamed of a shorebird flock. I fell back to sleep again and heard many songbirds singing. Nevada County has no records of Glaucous Gull, little shorebird habitat, and songbirds rarely sing in the fall. Dream birds do not count on a Big Day.

At dawn a Great Horned Owl called. The foothill camp, full of vehicles the night before, was empty. It was deer-hunting season and the hunters had all left before dawn. Since we did not want to be mistaken for deer, we decided not to cross the creek and walk up into the grassland to listen for birds. Instead, we walked along the main road. As the light increased there were sparrows in the brush and a late Tree Swallow overhead.

1. Kenn Kaufman, *Kingbird Highway* (Boston, MA, Houghton Mifflin Co., 1997) 174.

Later that morning we found a migrating Pacific-slope Flycatcher among the oaks of a nearby town park, and then we fell behind schedule looking for other migrants. It was time to leave the foothills. If we had scouted, maybe we would have known where a California Thrasher skulked and where those oak woodland birds were that we missed. Hard-core birders scout the day or week before; but, then, elite athletes always train and plot harder. Our own goal was to see a hundred species, and to do that we needed to get to the mountains: new habitats.

In the mid-afternoon we were surprised to find some Common Terns, uncommon for the region, sitting on a sandbar in a reservoir. In a nearby tree we were relieved to find our first Yellow-rumped Warbler of the day, the most common fall warbler in Northern California. We finished with ninety-five birds. If only we had scouted the day before—and not taken that forty minute detour to that pond with no birds—we might have found five more. If only the official ABA rule was that 95% of the birds on our list had to be seen or heard by at least one participant!

Next year. We are luckier than those brief-lived insects. We can do as many Big Days as we want.

Keeping Lists is another game birders play. Each checked bird on a list confirms a possibility. Each unchecked bird is an unfulfilled wish. There are lists for when birds were seen—day, trip, year, life list; and for where birds were seen—yard, park, county, state, country, continent. Lists with dates, locations, and numbers of birds seen or heard can provide valuable data if a species' status and distribution starts to change; but most lists are primarily for their listers. Some birders also keep idiosyncratic lists—birds seen on telephone wires, birds seen or heard on television, birds seen while attending a sporting event. There are many ways to play the game. When we play, we see more birds.

Birders can also play games with their lists. For the past two decades I have played a county birding game with a few friends. Could we see or hear one hundred birds in each of California's fifty-eight counties? We did, and then we decided the game was too much fun to stop. Could we see or hear one hundred and fifty birds in each county? Now the game was harder. We had to learn more about the status and distribution of birds in California. We had to go to specific habitats in each county in different seasons and look for particular birds we did not have yet. In other words, we had to go birding! Storms of winter raptors in Surprise Valley; a roadrunner lollygagging through the motel grounds in Anza Borrego; shorebird migration at Lake Tahoe—the game has no end. The current champion county lister in California has at least 225 birds in each county!

One fall day Helen and I tracked down a California Towhee near the American River. The towhee lives in both our yards but neither of us had seen it in Sacramento County. Driving two hours to see a bird we can see out our windows is silly, but our game had rules. Two weeks later I returned to Sacramento County and saw a large, immature accipiter land in a tree and then fly off. I needed both Sharp-shinned and Cooper's Hawk for that county, but which was it? If the bird was a Cooper's Hawk, which is common there in the fall, no one would doubt me. But I did not count the bird; I might be wrong. We county listers have to be our own fact-checkers and referees. And then, a few minutes later, above a soaring Red-tailed Hawk, a smaller hawk appeared with a long, rounded tail and a large-headed appearance. Cooper's Hawk! I put it on my county list.

If listing can sometimes turn birding into an obsession, that should not be a surprise. A few love affairs do end in stalking. Dan Koeppel, writing about his father's immense lists, said that seeing seven thousand birds "required a specific mindset: singular, focused, and obsessed, often to the point of blotting out anything—family, career, other pastimes—that might slow the quest."[1] His father said that listing birds was "an addiction, just like any other addiction. I can't explain it. I can't even say it ever gave me a sense of euphoria. It's just what I do."[2] Even if there were Birder's Anonymous meetings throughout the country, most birdaholics would not be in recovery. They might go to the meetings, but only to trade stories—and lists.

Although list-keeping is somewhat disreputable among nonbirders, who assume that such birders only want to add a bird to their list and not enjoy the bird itself, most birders I have met enjoy the bird and add it to their list. As Rick Taylor has written, "Listing birds ... represents our desire not just to enrich our lives, but also to organize our lives into a series of interlocking vignettes that ... are, if you will, the wings of memory..."[3]

The Salton Sea, in southeastern California, has a bird list of over four hundred species, including more species of waterbirds than any other part of the state. Tropical storms even push pelagic birds to the inland sea, directly north of the Gulf of California. Many birders have hit the bird jackpot there.

We wanted to try our luck at the Salton Sea, so one mid-January morning we left Los Angeles early and reached the sea's north end by 9 o'clock. The desert, often cool and windy in winter, was calm and warm. We set up our scopes and found more Snowy

---

1. Dan Koeppel, *To See Every Bird on Earth: A Father, a Son, and a Lifelong Obsession* (New York, Plume, 2006) xiv.

2. Koeppel, xvii.

3. Rick Taylor, "On Listing" (*Birding*, American Birding Association, 2004) 50-51.

Plovers than we were used to seeing in Northern California. We also saw a dead egret beneath some dying trees. The Salton Sea has no outlet. Pesticide-contaminated run-off from the surrounding farms and toxic discharges into the New River, flowing north from Mexicali, pollute the sea. Was the dead bird a bad omen?

We drove south along the east side of the sea. Two thousand Snow Geese fed in a bright green agricultural field near the Imperial Wildlife Area. From a distance, until I saw some stretch their wings, they looked like gigantic white vegetables. We followed directions to some trees where other birders had reported a Reddish Egret, rare in the state. All we saw were Snowy Egrets. A bird tour van stopped. The leader said the rare egret was "at the next tree down the road." We hurried down and found the tree but not the bird.

We looked for an hour and left but, after unenthusiastically studying a shorebird flock a few miles farther on, decided to return and look again. The egret was still not there. Then, as we debated how long we should wait, a Reddish Egret flew over our heads and landed in the grove of trees where we had first looked for it. Bingo!

Before they hit bottom, addicts assume they are in control of their lives. We now supposed the odds of seeing rare birds were in our favor. We were wrong. The next morning we missed a possible Anhinga, a super-lotto rare bird in California if confirmed, that other birders had been reporting at a lagoon a few miles north of the Mexican border. Instead we saw many Anhinga-like cormorants drying their wings.

I am glad the Salton Sea is a 9-10 hour drive from my San Francisco Bay Area home. If I lived closer, I would spend a lot of time playing the odds there. I am not a Big Lister but, as Mark Obmascik wrote, "The truth is that everyone has obsessions. Most people manage them. Birders, however, indulge them."[1]

---

1. Mark Obmascik, *The Big Year: A Tale of Man, Nature, and Fowl Obsession* (New York, Free Press, 2004) xiii.

One bird game that is easier to play than a Big Day, and speedier than keeping a list, is the Chase. A bird chase starts with a phone call or an Internet posting. There is usually only one bird, it is rare for that location, and finding it is chancy. Some birders think that chasing turns the joys of birding into yet another obsession. I enjoy a chase. I like the excitement of the hunt, and I savor finding the bird.

Sometimes I have driven to where the bird was last reported and have found a whole group of birders looking at it: instant gratification. Sometimes I have driven to where the bird was last reported, seen no one else, and found the bird myself, a more satisfying accomplishment. Sometimes I have never found the bird. At first I look at every bird eagerly. Then I look at every bird—but with less optimism. Is the bird still there and I just cannot find it? Has it long since flown? Will the bird show up again as soon as I leave? Is that what rear-view mirrors really are for?

One winter morning we chased a reported Snow Bunting across an old corn field near Humboldt Bay. The bunting was supposed to be with Lapland Longspurs. When we finally got close to the flock, all we saw were longspurs. They walked rapidly between the corn stalks and soon flushed to another part of the field. A local birder arrived. We asked him about the Snow Bunting. He said no one had seen a bunting there that year. We had been chasing a misidentification.

That night we called one of the local bird experts. He said the man we had met had seen, after we left, the Dickcissel that had been frequenting the corn field for the past few weeks and possibly a Smith's Longspur. He said some Humboldt Bay birders were going out to the corn field the next morning to look for the longspur.

Our chase was on again. Both birds would be state birds for each of us. When we got to the corn field a few local birders were already there. They had already seen the Dickcissel! One man showed us a digital picture of it. The bird was with the longspurs, but the flock had flown to another part of the field.

More birders arrived. We slowly approached the long-spur flock. It flew. We walked to where it had landed. A few more people saw the Dickcissel. I did not. One expert birder even apologized for seeing it, saying he was just "lucky." I silently disagreed. Better birders see more birds because they are more skillful, not luckier. The flock took off and flew around the corn field as I pleaded with it not to fly completely away. After more than five minutes of circling, the flock landed.

The birds walked in the furrows, rarely stood still, and flushed when we got close to them. Would I ever see the Dickcissel? Eventually we herded the flock into a corner of the field. As I searched for the bird that was not-a-longspur, two birders calmly announced they had the Dickcissel in their scopes. I walked over to them and one let me look. A gray, yellow, and black bird with a large, conical bill was pecking at one of the few corn cobs left in the field. The chase was over. I returned to my scope and stared at the most beautiful Dickcissel I had ever seen.

Another bird game I play is to try to see all the birds that regularly occur in California. Pete Dunne has written, "As skills grow, the sense of wonder that supports beginning birders diminishes. What replaces it is discovery. ... It is not as great as wonder. But it is very close, and it is also very addictive. Once a birder has a taste for it, there is only one thing that can satisfy the craving. And that is *more*."[1]

Snow Bunting is still on my yet-to-see state list, along with some other land birds. So are many seabirds. Since a birder's California extends two hundred miles out into the Pacific Ocean,

1. Pete Dunne, *The Feather Quest: A North American Birder's Year* (New York, Dutton, 1992) 45.

seeing pelagic birds is part of this game. Murphy's Petrel once was on that list. It took me more than ten years to see it.

Each spring I knew the bird was out there, but each spring I was stuck on land. Either there was no spring boat trip out of Northern California, where I live; or the trip did not go far enough off shore to where the bird usually stays, which is more than thirty miles out; or work and family came first; or I was unlucky—bad weather canceled one long distance spring trip. The bird had been seen closer to shore off of Fort Bragg, a four-hour drive up the coast, so one year I took a boat trip from there. We saw five hundred Black-footed Albatrosses but no Murphy's Petrel.

Then my luck changed. A four-night trip out of San Diego, heading a hundred and twenty miles into the Pacific, had Murphy's Petrel as one of its target species. Once on board *The Searcher* I learned that Murphy's Petrel was on a lot of most-wanted bird lists. Only a few of us twenty-eight birders had ever seen one.

Our captain said the horizon was about ten miles from the main deck. He said on a clear day we could scan for birds about two miles in every direction, but it is impossible to identify a bird two miles away. We needed Murphy's Petrel to come to us. Since many pelagic birds rely on their sense of smell to find food, we tossed chum off the stern of the boat. Our chum was a potently odoriferous mix of popcorn and tuna oil. We hoped a distant Murphy's Petrel would smell it and detour to our boat to investigate.

On the second afternoon we put out a tuna oil-and-popcorn slick at the Rodriguez Sea Mount. The birders on last week's boat had seen the bird here. I did not have to wonder for long if I would jinx us. Almost immediately someone shouted, "Murphy's Petrel." I jumped to my feet. There! A sleek bat of a bird swerved and swooped upwards, sideways, and downwards above the waves. The bird looked larger than its almost three-foot wing span, as if it had grown in my mind each year I had not seen it. I had read about its flight but had not understood that if most birds have mastered the basics, Murphy's Petrel is a grandmaster, able to perform aerial maneuvers most other birds would never attempt. Then, like some phantom, it was gone.

To my surprise, the exhilaration at seeing Murphy's Petrel was soon diluted by a sense of loss. I no longer had a bird to look for, and there were two full days of birding left. I wanted "more." Cook's Petrel and Red-billed Tropicbird were both regular off the coast of Southern California in the spring, though, and I had not seen either bird in California waters. Two Red-billed Tropicbirds had been reported on the previous week's trip list. I began to scan the ocean again.

Early the next morning a few people heard two tropicbirds call in the dark and saw two silhouettes fly over the boat's light. I was still sleeping. We saw about a hundred birds that day—not species, birds. There were a few Black-footed Albatrosses, some Northern Fulmars, and small flocks of Red Phalaropes. A few more Murphy's Petrels roller-coasted by. But the lack of birds was not discouraging. When there are lots of common birds, the next one will probably be another common one. When there are only a few birds, surely the next one will be a Cook's Petrel or a Red-billed Tropicbird: birder's logic.

The following day the captain spotted a tropicbird on the water. We all rushed to the bow. One woman, in the shower when she heard the announcement, rushed on deck with dripping wet hair. A Red-billed Tropicbird floated near the boat for a few minutes before flying off. We all got great looks: proof of birder's logic.

I also have made up my own bird-games. One spring my wife and I went to Caruthers Canyon, in the high desert of southeastern California, twenty-plus miles south of the interstate, a few miles west down a side road and a few hundred yards north into the canyon itself. No one goes there on the way to anywhere else. Birders go there because the high desert is full of birds in May and June. As we set up our tent and made supper, I wished for morning so I could go birding. What was here? Before the sun came up I was walking among the cacti.

Maybe my mind began to wander because I was alone with the birds, or maybe it was because of the Scott's Orioles. There were about thirty of them. As I dawdled and gawked at

Scott's Oriole

29

the males' regal black and yellow coats, I began to pretend the orioles were kings and queens of an avian Shangri-La. Whenever I saw one, I bowed. I imagined the orioles were holding court on top of the ocotillos and the juniper trees, and were granting me a brief audience before they flew to a more distant perch. When the day warmed up and the birds slowed down, I returned to camp and told Carol that the Scott's Orioles were the canyon's royalty. She was more interested in seeing and hearing an oriole than in hearing my story, but play always means most to the players.

I did not play fantasy birding all the time. For three mornings I also improved my birding skills. Not being able to recognize a bird's call note meant there was a mystery bird to follow. An unidentified chip beneath a juniper became a Le Conte's Thrasher. A female hummingbird became a Costa's when it landed near me.

Steve Howell has written, "I once heard it said that a good birder is someone who enjoys birding."[1] I enjoyed birding Caruthers Canyon. The last morning, as I said goodbye to the orioles, I wondered what other bird games I could play. Maybe how many birds I could show my grandchildren.

---

1. Steven N.G. Howell, "Letters to the Editor" (*Birding*, American Birding Association, 2004) 457–458.

Surprises

One July Helen and I decided to see some birds we were unlikely ever to see in the San Francisco Bay Area, so we drove south to the Audubon California Kern River Preserve. It was over a hundred degrees when we arrived. As we looked for a picnic table in the shade, an all-red bird landed briefly in a nearby tree. Summer Tanager! It is one of the Kern River Valley specialties and very local in the rest of the state.

I was glad to see it but shared Peter Cashwell's reaction after he followed directions to a rare bird. "[I] felt both curiously unsatisfied and mystified by my lack of satisfaction ... I had almost immediately found the bird I'd been after ... But I still [found] it wanting in one quality: surprise."[1] Mark Cocker explains, "For most birders there is only one thing better than seeing good birds. You can probably guess what it is ... it's actually finding the thing for yourself."[2] Yes. We had hoped to see the tanager. And we did. But I wanted a bird to surprise me.

The Kern Valley is also known for its many southbound hummingbirds that stop and feed there each summer, and as we ate lunch we watched the activity at the many feeders hung near the visitor's center. One male Rufous Hummingbird shimmered in the sunlight with a golden veneer. I stared at what may have been the most gorgeous bird I have ever seen. It was a taste of surprise.

1. Peter Cashwell, *The Verb 'To Bird': Sightings of an Avid Birder* (Philadelphia, PA, Paul Dry Books, 2003) 82.

2. Mark Cocker, *Birders: Tales of a Tribe* (New York, Atlantic Monthly Press, 2001) 132.

The riparian corridor along the Kern River is surrounded by a Joshua Tree high desert plateau, and that evening I studied desert birds in the field guide. In the morning we drove a few miles south and walked up a dry wash past some juniper trees. A pair of Black-Throated Sparrows were calling and feeding their young. A Cactus Wren sang from atop a Joshua Tree flower pod. The field guide had come to life.

Then we switchbacked three thousand feet up out of the valley and into the southern Sierra. At the BLM Chimney Creek Campground, a hand-written sign at the entrance asked for donations to fix the leaking water system. But with the water leaking, what a great place for birds! A puzzling call turned out to be a soon-to-fledge Cooper's Hawk in its nest. Another glowing male Rufous Hummingbird was at the camp host's feeders.

Don't all birders go through the same developmental stages? First, we want to see new birds. More precisely, we want to see all the birds in the book; whether someone shows them to us or not, we just want to see them. When I started birding and took classes with Joe Morlan at the City College of San Francisco, all the birds I had never seen were rare to me. After seeing a new bird on one of his field trips I would look at its picture and compare that with the bird I just saw.

If we keep birding, though, just seeing or hearing new birds is not enough. We do want to find them ourselves, the rarer the better. Gradually we come to understand what Kenn Kaufman meant when he wrote, "There is nothing like being there at the initial discovery ... that heart-pounding, short-of-breath realization that this bird is something completely unexpected. Such moments are rare in the lives of most birders, but the mere hope for them adds spice to many an hour in the field."[1]

1. Kenn Kaufman, *Flights Against the Sunset* (Boston, MA, Houghton Mifflin Co., 2008) 30.

On our way back across the Sierra, by a creek, we found a small flock of Lawrence's Goldfinch. Were they rare here? We thought they only occurred at lower elevations. No, the guide book said, but for a few moments we thought we had found an unexpected bird all by ourselves. Maybe next trip.

If birding is a kind of love, it follows that no effort to find birds is too strenuous or feels too unlikely to succeed. I backpacked in six miles to search for the Black Swifts that had nested at a waterfall in the Trinity Alps the previous year. They were not there. It was mildly disappointing, but I was on the edge of hope for two days. And my trips to Clark Mountain, almost 8000 feet high in the eastern Mojave, had me excited for months before we left. Birds that occur regularly in southeast Arizona occasionally wander across the desert in spring and land in the white fir forest near the mountain's top. We were going to look for rare vagrants.

There are no signs at Clark Mountain that direct visitors to a trailhead, because there is no trail. On my first visit, many years ago, with my friends Robin and Frank, we did not even know where to start climbing, our maps were so inadequate. We stopped at a gas station on Interstate 5 to ask directions. Tacked to the wall behind the counter was a newspaper photo of a long, thick snake. The caption said it was the local Mojave Green Rattlesnake and could kill by poison or paralysis because it had two kinds of venom. I kept staring at the picture as the man told us about a nearby mining road that led to where we could camp at the foot of the mountain.

The road ended at a small open area with a picnic table. The slope above was covered with what looked like an impenetrable growth of short trees and bushes. We could not see a way up the mountain, but it was late afternoon and we decided to spend the night there. Robin and Frank slept in their van.

Grace's Warbler

There was no level place to pitch my tent and, remembering the picture of the snake, I put my sleeping bag on top of the table. The next day we followed a partially overgrown path. It soon ended in a dense thicket. We could not get to the white fir forest from here; we could not even see any firs.

The next year I went back with Helen, her husband Paul, and better directions to the real birders' base camp. It was on the other side of the mountain. At the first hint of light we found a dry stream bed and started our ascent. We could see the white firs above us and reached them in a few hours. We saw an Hepatic Tanager, a rare summer resident. We heard a song we did not recognize: Grace's Warbler! A vagrant! We had "found the thing" ourselves.

George Levine has written "I expect that everyone who dabbles in birding ... will value birding in ways that ramify out into their lives complexly, often secretly."[1] Although we did not slay a dragon or have a vision on Clark Mountain, we had avoided the dangerous snake, found the hidden passage, and stumbled on the treasure.

We went back the next year, found an Hepatic Tanager again, but could not find any vagrants. Quests are not always successful. After birding the white fir forest, Paul and I climbed to the top of the mountain and looked out over the desert. We could see the freeway. I thought about returning to that gas station and giving them a picture of Grace's Warbler to tack up next to the rattler. And maybe a map.

1. George Levine, *Lifebirds*, (New Brunswick, NJ, Rutgers University Press, 1955) 5.

Seeing an owl is always a surprise. Their round faces, vowel-laden voices, and night flight make them seem like distant relatives who send postcards now and then from strange places. Owls embody the attractiveness of the exotic. To hear or see an owl, we have to be owl-like ourselves. We have to focus our attention on the night sounds and make our ears big and empty. We have to whistle or hoot like an owl to coax it toward us so it can investigate the other "owl" in its territory.

I went with Robin and Frank in early December to Robinson Canyon, near Monterey; six species of owls live there. We arrived at dusk, parked at a turnout, and started walking up the narrow road that winds through the deciduous and fir forest. It was a cool night. There was no wind. The sweater I put on over my jacket muffled the noise I made when I moved my arms. I kept reminding myself that the sound of air passing through my nostrils was not a forest noise.

As we walked we took turns imitating a Northern Saw-whet Owl—lots of whistled notes on the same pitch. If an owl called and it was close to us, we would shine our flashlights in the direction of the sound. If we saw eye shine we would be looking at the owl. After a few minutes a distant saw-whet answered! A few minutes later another distant saw-whet answered! Neither bird flew in.

We drove up the canyon. Every few hundred yards we stopped to whistle. No owl responded. We turned around at the top and stopped to whistle every few hundred yards back down the canyon. No owl responded. Surrounded by silence and unable to see, we could have been in outer space.

Robin and Frank have a house in a small canyon about five miles away. Western Screech-Owls live there. We returned to their home and played an owl tape from their deck. I assumed a resident screech-owl would immediately answer, since it would certainly hear this intruder. No owl responded. Before going to bed I opened the window, despite the cold, so I could hear a screech-owl if one did call. A distant Great Horned Owl hooted just before I turned off the light.

It was dark when I woke and went outside to listen, hoping I had a date with a screech-owl. I heard the wind, a wind chime, some crickets, and a car. I heard a branch scratch against the downspout, a distant dog bark, and a distant duck quack. As it got light and tree silhouettes appeared, the first Wrentit bounced its song down the canyon and I went back inside. The screech-owl—and three others!—had stood me up.

Middle-aged bird-love is different than adolescent bird-love, and the passage through middle-age can be as perilous as a bird's migration. When the dreams of youth and young adulthood start to fade, the desire for new experiences can increase exponentially. Birders are lucky. We do not have to have an affair or take up rollerblading; we can take a bird trip.

I have been taking pelagic trips off the coast of Northern California for the past thirty years and being on the ocean always holds the promise of surprises. One November day on the Cordell Bank a juvenile Short-tailed Albatross landed near our boat and ate popcorn chum with some Black-footed Albatrosses. At that time it was only the third record off the coast of California in the twentieth century. It was a much bigger bird than the black-footeds. It had a huge bubble-gum pink bill and looked like a winged giant from another planet, which was almost true. The bird had spent most of its life at sea.

The trip's leader, Rich Stallcup, author of a guide to Pacific Coast pelagic birds, shouted "Short-tailed Albatross" in a loud, incredulous voice and then bounced around the boat as if he was trying to fly over to the bird and introduce himself. We were all still bird-high when the boat docked. Helen remembers doing a jig-step in the parking lot and watching Rich do one, too.

Twenty years later, I was on another of Rich's pelagic trips to the Cordell Bank. Birds were unusually scarce all morning. People chatted. Some watched the gulls that were following the boat and eating the chum that was meant to attract shearwaters, storm-petrels, and albatrosses. Others dozed in the sun. Then a dark bird, one that looked at first like a not unexpected Flesh-footed Shearwater, landed close to the boat. When it flew we could see its legs and feet were black. Rich immediately called out *Procellaria*. I had never heard that word. The bird landed. We approached and were able to study and photograph a Parkinson's Petrel. It was the first record for North America. If we had not been so flabbergasted, we all might have danced a jig around the boat.

We do not have to go out on a boat for a birding surprise. The finch we saw on our summer vacation can appear unexpectedly at our winter feeder. The lake or path we bird every week can surprise us with a bird we have never seen there before. Many years ago, before a September trip to Point Reyes National Seashore, I telephoned the Rare Bird Alert. Birders had seen rare birds there the day before. Helen and I hoped some of those rarities had spent the night.

Many had. My notes say we saw six vagrant warblers in the Monterey cypress at the Point Reyes ranches. I do not remember any of them. My notes also say that, in the willows, we saw a lime-green immature Chestnut-sided Warbler that no one had previously reported and a Black-billed Cuckoo. I only vaguely remember them, even though that warbler and cuckoo were life birds. What I do remember is how surprised I was to see so many birds that were not supposed to be there. Rare birds leave, but surprises can last forever.

Birds have a unique relationship with humans because they share our lives in ways that other groups of wildlife species do not. Because of their unique status in human societies, the protection and restoration of bird populations and habitats demands and deserves special emphasis among our conservation efforts. Fortunately, these efforts will directly benefit the environment and habitats shared by virtually all other species—including ours.

 The North American Bird Conservation Initiative
in the United States

Conservation

Our predecessors fought to protect migrating birds, to protect habitats, and to ban awful toxins from our environment. The ongoing revolution in field guides and optical equipment has allowed us to move from shooting a bird in order to study it to merely looking at it through binoculars or clicking a camera. Shooting what we love never did make sense. Our imagination and our conscience have also expanded. We do not put wild bird feathers on hats anymore.

Even so, the multi-agency State of the Birds 2009 Report found that approximately a third of all native birds in the United States are now either endangered, threatened, or species of conservation concern. Jonathan Rosen has written, "Birdwatching ... is the real national pastime, it just isn't televised. In fact, though, it is more than the national pastime, because the field of play is the earth itself. We are the players and the spectators. And the outcome—since bird and watcher are intimately connected—is literally a matter of life and death."[1]

For this reason, when I learn about a new wildlife refuge or public-private land trust agreement that protects "undeveloped" land, I feel stubbornly optimistic. With enough open space, many of the bird species we live with might continue to live with us. When I learn how birders' sightings collected on eBird are helping focus conservation efforts, it makes me want to be a more active citizen-scientist.

Along with many other birders across the continent, I have played a small role in a bird-protection program by censusing

1. Jonathan Rosen, *The Life of the Skies* (New York, Farrar, Straus and Giroux, 2008) 121.

for a Breeding Bird Atlas (BBA). The object of a BBA is to determine whether a species possibly, probably, or definitely breeds in a five-by-five kilometer block. It is not enough to see a bird; the species has to show evidence of breeding behavior. BBAs let a birder contribute to science, datum by datum.

As I censused, birding became a spectator sport, too. I rooted for and pleaded with the birds I was watching to show me they were nesting. When I observed an adult bird carrying nesting material or food in its beak, or heard and then watched a recently fledged bird begging for food, I silently cheered, as if we all were on the same team.

I also wanted the nestlings to be safe from raccoons, crows, and jays, and the fledglings to be safe from hawks. When I returned to my area a few years later I saw many of the same species. Were some of them the very same birds I had watched and cheered? Migratory birds sometimes return and nest in the same tree. Had some of these birds hatched here? If my grandchildren came here as adults would these same species still be here? I wish all kids could participate in a BBA as part of their elementary school science curriculum. They would not only learn bird identification and general observation skills, they also would learn to care about what happened to their local birds and habitats. Maybe some of them would grow up to be passionate birders.

Changes in habitat, even slight or subtle ones, affect where or even whether birds breed. Some species benefit from them, others do not. Fifty years ago Chestnut-backed Chickadees were rare in my block. Now they are common breeders. But Loggerhead Shrikes used to breed in my block, and now they are gone.

The imaginary glass of birds is neither half-full nor half-empty. It is badly cracked. If we cannot fix it, the variety of bird species and the number of birds of many species will continue to decrease. Eventually some species will disappear. If we want to keep birds around us, we have to preserve their habitats.

Alexander Skutch can help us here. He wrote about birds, "The more profoundly and sympathetically we study them, the stronger grows our intuition that they are conscious, until it becomes a certainty, and the less remote from us they appear. A first consequence of our growing rapport with them is their inclusion in the sphere of our ethical concern; we treat them as creatures that enjoy and suffer, not as insentient objects."[1] William Dawson came to a similar conclusion about the minds of birds: "And be assured that the birds are full of 'human nature'; that is, they are enough like us in behavior to be understandable. ... They show as between themselves these psychological differences which connote individuality. They are always bird persons."[2] Donald Kroodsma did, too. After a lifetime of studying birdsong, he reached "an inescapable truism: my aesthetic tastes and those of many birds must overlap."[3]

Intuitions are not the same as scientific claims, but we make them about each other and act on them with conviction in our daily lives. Insofar as we trust our intuitions, we will love birds, and if we love them, we will protect their habitats—we care for what we love.

One May, while driving in the Tule Lake National Wildlife Refuge with my wife, I stopped the car because five Violet-green Swallows were standing in the middle of the road. When we looked more closely, we saw a dead swallow near them, presumably hit by another car. One swallow kept approaching the dead bird and poking at it with its beak. The birds did not fly even when we approached to within ten feet of them. The conclusion that the birds felt their loss struck us as inescapable.

1. Alexander F. Skutch, *The Minds of Birds* (College Station, TX, Texas A and M University Press, 1996) 164.

2. William Leon Dawson, *The Birds of California, Vol. 2* (San Diego, CA, South Moulton Co., 1923) 738–739.

3. Donald Kroodsma, *The Singing Life of Birds* (Boston, MA, Houghton Mifflin Co., 2005) 275.

Look what we did for the condor. During the 1970s a debate simmered about whether to capture the few remaining wild California Condors and attempt to breed them in captivity or let them become extinct—because there seemed to be too little habitat left to support them. I was on the side of leaving them alone. Great Auk, Passenger Pigeon, California Condor: maybe the extinct condor, once so widespread, could be an especially potent symbol to inspire us to work harder to protect habitat for birds.

Now I think I was wrong. Captive breeding was successful, California Condors have been re-introduced into the wild, and re-introduced condors out there are a better symbol than pictures and memories for what we can do to save bird species, if we really try. True, the re-introduced condors are not "purely" wild. We have a name and number for each one, and if we don't feed them at stake-outs we risk losing them again. But many species depend on us to protect their habitat; condors just require more efforts than most. Many species are the "condors" of the future, even more crowded world.

One April weekend my wife and I drove down the Big Sur coast with some friends who knew the area well. We stopped at a pull-out overlooking the ocean, and they said this was a place where they sometimes saw a condor soaring in the afternoon wind. We looked up and, sure enough, soon saw one. It was huge, with a black-and-white pattern unlike that of any other bird. I felt moved by its magnificence and also by the fact that a condor was still—again—flying over the California coast.

A Turkey Vulture appeared, big but puny compared to the condor, and then a Peregrine Falcon began circling above us. At one time I had the condor, the peregrine, and the vulture in the same binocular view. Without our help, neither the condor nor the falcon would have been there, and without them—with just the vulture up there—the sky would have been far duller.

What is it like to touch a bird? I once touched a dead hummingbird on our porch. At first I did not want to pick it up. Then I did not want to put it down. Maybe it was magical thinking, that if I kept holding onto the bird it would revive and fly away.

Bird banders care for birds by touching them. I wanted to watch them at work, so one morning I visited the Coyote Creek Field Station. The banders' code of ethics states that their work must be "beyond reproach," and that "banders are responsible for the safety and welfare of the birds they study." These Coyote Creek banders even had to take fox precautions because, if they did not remove a netted bird soon enough, it might become an easy meal for one of the resident gray foxes.

After the nets were put in place, one bander started on fox patrol. If she found a netted bird she would use her walkie-talkie to tell the other two where it was. The other two banders planned to return to their small field station and, every half hour come back to check the nets, but before they could even leave, the nets had caught five birds.

Helen was one of the banders. She untangled a Song Sparrow, put it in a small cloth bag, and pulled the drawstring shut so the bird could not escape. I accompanied her back to the field station, where she hung the bag on a wall hook next to the four other bags, which held two more Song Sparrows and two Lincoln's Sparrows. The bags moved when the birds fluttered.

The banders put on magnifying goggles. One by one, they each took a bird out of its bag. They held the bird with its head between their first and second fingers, its legs up, their hand cupping its back. If the bird had been previously caught and banded, they recorded the band number. If the bird had not been caught before, they put a new band around one of the bird's legs with a pair of special pliers. They determined its age and sex, if possible, measured the length of its primary and secondary wing feathers, and recorded all these data while holding the bird. Next they put the bird in a little tube and weighed it. Finally they took the bird outside and let it go. Each released bird would become a doubly valuable source of information if it were recaptured, as the passage of time would be added to the data matrix.

Beyond the data-gathering, maybe to touch a bird is to be touched by that bird. When Helen spread a Hermit Thrush's wing and told me that the buffy tips on the primaries suggested a second-year bird, her voice had a slight sparkle. If I were a bander, I would wear a bird-band on my finger.

John Hay wrote "So it is their constant presence, and at the same time their elusiveness, which intrigues us."[1] When the feeder is full, the resident or visiting finches, and perhaps a hummingbird, join our family. Feeders make birds less elusive. A hawk's appearance can turn a routine breakfast into a memorable meal for us, and sometimes for the hawk.

Cats are a problem we bring to the birds' world. They kill a million birds a day in North America. I don't have a bird feeder because I could not convince my family to keep our cat indoors. We put a bell on her so the birds could hear her coming and fly before she pounced. Even so, when she was young she killed a Lincoln's Sparrow. I felt like a villain.

Helen is a better bird neighbor. She has kept feeders filled in her backyard for many years and currently runs a three-star avian restaurant. She chases the neighborhood cats away. Two feeders hang from a ten-foot copper pole; another pole supports a rectangular platform feeder. She also has a hummingbird

1. John Hay, *The Great House of Birds* (San Francisco, CA, Sierra Club Books, 1996) xii.

feeder, a wire cage with suet suspended from her birch tree, and a water fountain. Her thirty-year yard list of over one hundred species includes permanent residents, migrants, waterbirds flying overhead to or from nearby San Francisco Bay, and even a few eastern vagrants.

I went to her house one drizzly, windy February morning when there were no birds in my front yard and watched from her kitchen window. Fifteen species came to dine in the next hour, including a hummingbird, two woodpeckers, two warblers, and three sparrows. Twice all the birds flew off and did not return for ten minutes. Helen said there was a Cooper's Hawk in the neighborhood. By noon much of the birdseed had been eaten. When our old cat dies, I'm going to put up a feeder and be a better bird neighbor.

Banders capture, tag, and release healthy birds. Wildlife rehabilitation specialists nurse injured birds back to health and raise abandoned chicks to maturity. Robin is the Species Manager of the hummingbird team at the Lindsay Wildlife Museum Hospital. When injured or abandoned hummingbirds are brought to the museum, the team members take them home and care for them until, all hope, the birds are strong enough to survive in the wild. For eighteen years Robin has successfully rehabbed hummingbirds.

She has little cages at home and an aviary in her backyard. If the hummingbird is only a few days old, she will feed it from a syringe filled with water, vitamins, and Vital Diet— a mixture used in hospitals for human patients who cannot digest their food. She does this every twenty minutes during the day, about the way an adult hummingbird would feed its young. If the bird is older—it takes 5-6 weeks for one to fledge—she feeds it Nectar Plus, a zoo diet for hummingbirds that she has enhanced with proteins.

As a surrogate parent, Robin experiences the pride or despair of all parents with each bird she tries to raise. When I asked her why she works so hard to rehab hummingbirds, she said it is how she makes amends to the Earth for all the deaths we cause so many other creatures. And she said it was rewarding: "When a hummingbird is in my house, I feel an intimacy with life itself. They are curious and intelligent. You can watch them think." She has saved a lot of hummingbird children.

I asked Robin if a hummingbird ever got out of its cage when she is feeding it. "Yes." How does she get it back? "I stand on a chair with a broom or a net and don't let it land. If the young bird has to keep hovering, soon enough it will tire and flutter to the ground or flop on the windowsill. Then I can net it." How did she think of that? Parents learn what works with their children.

Robin told me she puts the young hummingbirds into her outdoor aviary as soon as she can and releases them as soon as she can after that. When she lets a hummingbird go in her backyard, it sometimes stays around for a few days, perhaps defending territory, at least feeding on her flowers. She likes that. Sometimes it's hard for parents when their grown children leave home.

Once in downtown Berkeley she was walking to the courthouse to file some papers when she heard a hummingbird, and then saw it flutter from a nearby tree to a restaurant terrace across the street. The bird could barely fly; it landed on a railing near a table. Robin crossed the street, easily approached the bird, and simply picked it up. It sat in her hand. She cupped it, with its beak sticking out between her fingers, and continued to the courthouse. She went through the metal (but apparently not hummingbird) detector and, with one hand, took papers out of her briefcase, filed them, and put the copies back in her briefcase. Her husband picked her up, and she brought the bird home. It was a Black-chinned Hummingbird, far from its preferred riparian habitat. A few weeks later, when it was able to fly farther than across a street, she released it near a riparian thicket in the delta.

I brought my youngest grandson, then not quite two, to see that hummingbird. Robin had two other young Anna's Hummingbird in her study. He stared intently at each bird. She took the Black-chinned out of its cage. As he reached out and touched it, he smiled—two youngsters, one with feathers, one with opposable thumbs, briefly connected.

*Their universal presence is one reason why birds have galvanised our interest like no other life form on earth ... But it doesn't actually tackle the whole issue of **why** birds. I think it's much more to do with freedom, with notions of flight and escape, with some of our deepest fantasies, even with eroticism.*

 Mark Cocker

Stories

When my oldest grandson was first learning to talk, he was intoxicated with words and would recite nouns whose only connection to each other was that he could say them. We clapped our hands and smiled at his verbal proficiency. Aren't birders just large toddlers with expensive optical equipment? We recite names of birds, whose only connection to each other is that we have or haven't seen them, to anyone who will listen.

Birding San Francisco Bay has made this grown-up toddler very happy, partly because thousands of ducks and shorebirds winter here or stop to feed during migration. On a walk one early spring morning I saw fifty species of birds in two hours. It was low tide. On the exposed mud flats, a few Ruddy Turnstones stood together on their bright orange legs beside the aptly-named Long-billed Curlew. Near shore, statuesque egrets stalked while ducks dabbled, and in the deeper water a tern hovered and dove near a flock of preening grebes. Later, when I told my wife about the male Cinnamon Teal in the marsh, she smiled. She knew that intensely red duck with its red eye because we had seen it together, and she knew she had missed a treat.

Its color makes the Cinnamon Teal one of the first birds a beginning birder notices in the field guide. Black Skimmer is another. A skimmer's huge, red, black-tipped bill, with its long lower mandible, makes me think it escaped from the pages of a bestiary. There is a small resident colony of skimmers in the south bay now, but twenty years ago a Black Skimmer sighting in San Francisco Bay made the bird-news. When I heard of one near my house, I chased it. When I showed my wife its picture in the field guide, she laughed out loud.

One of these days I am going to take my grandsons to see the skimmers. The youngest one is starting to talk and now we marvel at his growing vocabulary. When they see their first skimmer, I bet they both will start talking about its beak. Whatever they say, I will smile. After all, I am their grandfather. If someone would listen to me and smile no matter what I said, probably I would talk about birds.

When my daughter, a teacher, asked me to show her kindergarten class some of the birds that lived near her school, I readily agreed. As Lyanda Lynn Haupt has written, "Birds will give you a window, if you allow them. They will show you secrets from another world, fresh vision that, though avian, can accompany you home and alter your life."[1] I wanted to give the children a glimpse of the bird world.

Twenty children were sitting on a rug, waiting for their teacher's father to arrive, when I entered the classroom. They immediately began to tell me the names of birds they had seen. I heard "duck," "goose," and "eagle." My daughter told them to take turns. A boy said he had seen a vulture, and another boy said he had seen a hawk carrying a fish in its claws. A girl said she had a hummingbird feeder at her house. One boy said they used to have a chicken in their classroom.

We went outside to a willow-lined creek next to the school's blacktop playground. My lesson plan was to show each child at least one bird. Since their attention was likely to be brief, I would need to show them that bird before they got restless. And since no one had binoculars, we would have to get close enough to that bird to see its color and shape and

1. Lyanda Lynn Haupt, *Rare Encounters with Ordinary Birds* (Seattle, WA, Sasquatch Books, 2001) 11.

watch what it was doing. I stopped to look and listen. Some of the children were talking. Two were pushing each other. I saw a Ruby-crowned Kinglet feeding in some low branches and led the class over to it. The bird was even more active than the children were, but nobody saw it. Some of the children began twisting their torsos and flapping their arms.

A robin landed high in a redwood tree, and a Yellow-rumped Warbler disappeared into the willows. I could not hope to show the children either bird. We flushed some sparrows from a bush. They flew into the next bush. This was my chance! But as I tried to get the children to sneak up on the sparrows, other classes flocked onto the playground for recess. The sparrows flew off. My daughter told her class that anyone who wanted to play could go. Most did.

I changed my lesson plan. Maybe I could show at least one child one bird. The few who stayed walked with me beneath the willows and looked up into the trees. Three Lesser Goldfinches were feeding less than ten feet away. Their yellow-green feathers and tiny cone-shaped bills were easy to see. The children stared. I had never been happier to see goldfinches. Then the bell rang. My bird class was over.

On the way home I hoped at least one child told his or her parents about those goldfinches. I also thought about "the hawk with a fish in its claws" that had impressed one of the boys. He sparked a memory of my own. Once I watched an adult Bald Eagle harass an Osprey until the Osprey dropped the large fish it had caught. The eagle tried three times to pick the floating fish off the water's surface but could not do it. The fish was too big. Then the eagle landed in the water, grabbed the fish with its talons, and rowed with its wings to a mud flat about fifty feet away. That was the only time I have seen an eagle row.

Why do we bird? Why, once they capture our attention, often in our childhood, do we so love birds? At each stage of life we answer the question differently. Birds are youthful novelties, mid-life escapes, and senior companions. When I was younger I was most interested in hard-to-find birds. I drove to Mount Pinos to look for condors before the last truly wild ones were captured. Eventually two birds soared past like small planes! They never flapped. I checked condor off my list. I drove more than three hours from Berkeley to Yosemite to look for a Great Gray Owl, did not see one, and drove back home the same day. My wife still remembers that wild owl chase.

I never birded like a love-struck adolescent, never drove all night and ate energy bars for breakfast, never checked every desert oasis in eastern California to see what vagrant might be there. I did not start birding until I was twenty-six and was still in the honeymoon phase the year the wind blew my tent down at Death Valley, and I had to spend a cramped night in the car. The next day my friend and I found a rare-in-the-state Upland Sandpiper on the Furnace Creek golf course, redeeming not only the bad night but also the whole trip.

A few years later I birded Butterbredt Springs in the dry foothills of the southern Sierra, much closer to where I live than Death Valley. A small pool surrounded by cattails and a trickle of water that meanders for a few hundred yards support a swatch of green that beckons any hungry or thirsty bird flying overhead. There is no place to camp, so I slept in my car. The next morning I overheard one young guy say to another that he had been on the ocean the weekend before and had seen Murphy's Petrel. I was birding with hard-core chasers that morning.

I wish I had been an adolescent birder. My checklists from those years with rare birds would contain romantic

Snow Geese

memories, and I would have forgotten the sleep deprivation and cold meals. Now that I am older, the sight of a meadowlark's lemon-yellow breast is more satisfying than it used to be, maybe because I have accepted that I am more meadowlark than Gyrfalcon.

Reminiscing about past birding moments is also more pleasurable now. Carol and I remember when a hummingbird nearly landed on her brightly colored bathing suit and when an owl answered her hooting. One late winter afternoon at the Sacramento Wildlife Refuge it started to drizzle as we stood on the viewing platform. The sun was in the west above the Coast Range. Looking east, we watched a rainbow appear and then a second rainbow. Flocks of Snow Geese called to each other as they flew beneath the dark gray clouds and the rainbows. We felt connected to—what?—life?

When my oldest grandson was three, a bird story became memorable in a way I had not anticipated. He wanted to "read books." When I had "read" to him from my bird guide, he had particularly liked the owls. That day he asked to see the picture of the Barn Owl again. I showed it to him and tried to imitate its shriek. He laughed. I showed him the Great Horned Owl. When I hooted its call loudly, he fussed. When I hooted softly, he smiled and said he wanted to "see it." We kept looking at pictures of owls and I kept imitating their calls. I told him that some of the owls lived in our local park and we could try to see them when he got a little older. When we came to the Flammulated Owl, I told him the story of what happened once when I tried to see it for myself.

—◦◦◦—

The Owl That Took My Sweater

One spring night at a car campground in the southern Sierra, a Flammulated Owl called. It was close to my tent. I looked for it with my flashlight but did not see it. When it stopped calling I went to sleep. At first light I woke to the owl calling. It was close to my tent again. I got dressed and went to look for it. It kept calling as it moved up a hill, and I followed. Pretty soon I took my sweater off and tied it around my waist. Eventually the owl stopped calling. I never did see it. Back in camp, while eating breakfast, I realized my sweater was gone. I climbed back up the hill and looked but never found my sweater.

When I got home I told Carol that an owl had taken the sweater she had given me. She laughed and said she could find me another sweater just like the one the owl took, and she did.

—◦◦◦—

I was wearing the second sweater when I told my grandson the story. At the end of the story, I pointed to the sweater and said the owl took a sweater just like this one. He liked that story. He asked me to tell it again. When I finished he asked me to tell it still again—eight times in a row. Which, of course, I did. After one telling, he said it was "silly" that the owl took my sweater. After another he said maybe the sweater was "in the dumpster" or "on the mantle." When his mother came home he told her an owl had taken my sweater. She laughed.

It's a five-hour drive from my home to the trailhead at Juniper Lake in Lassen Volcanic National Park, and an easy three-mile walk to Snag Lake, where my wife and I honeymooned, where we spent many subsequent summer vacations, and where I have co-led a Golden Gate Audubon Society backpack birding trip with Robin for the past thirty years. I can close my eyes and see the birds of Snag Lake.

At first I wanted to know what birds were there and searched each micro-habitat for different species. Now, a hundred and sixty Lassen birds later, my notes tell me how common, uncommon, or rare each bird is at Snag Lake in August and September. I do not expect to add many new ones to my personal Lassen list. I know the wet grass where the snipe hides, the stump where the kestrel likes to perch, and the lava tumble where the Rock Wrens feed. If you bird somewhere regularly enough, the common birds become satisfying and a rare one stupefying.

Each morning at Snag Lake, we bird before breakfast. Finches call overhead and sometimes a Pygmy Owl hoots. To watch warblers, we sit on a fallen lodgepole trunk near where a willow overhangs a shallow pool. Birds fly into the willow and work their way down to the water to bathe and drink. It's a treat to see the brightly colored and finely patterned warblers at eye level instead of high in a tree.

Snag Lake meadow
Lassen Volcanic National Park

Before lunch we walk to the west side of the lake, where a fire burned part of the forest. Woodpeckers feed on the blackened trunks and Mountain Bluebirds perch on the snags. A few years after the fire a huge migrating flock of Rufous Hummingbirds—Robin estimated there were a thousand—fed on the flowering dogbane that covered the recently scorched hillside.

After dinner we sit in the meadow and watch the night arrive. A Bald Eagle flies towards its nest on the west ridge. Five or six Common Nighthawks appear out of nowhere. Once one swooped so close to us I heard the whoosh of its wings and ducked, though I never saw it.

On our twenty-fourth annual trip, as we sat on the fallen log one morning and watched the birds come to the willow near the water, Janet, a long-time member of our group, suddenly said she was looking at "something different and I don't know what it is." I turned and saw a Chestnut-sided Warbler, rare in California and completely unexpected at Snag Lake. It flew to a nearby lodgepole pine; with my heart pounding, I watched it for a minute or so before it disappeared into the forest. After a hundred and fifty mornings of sitting on that log and looking at birds in that willow, we had found an eastern warbler in Lassen Volcanic National Park!

At 6:45 on a late May morning the temperature was 34 degrees at the Lower Klamath Wildlife Refuge. If the birds were cold, I couldn't tell, though my finger tips were as I watched a flock of Franklin's Gulls—a state bird for me—feeding in a field beneath snow-covered Mount Shasta. Iridescent ibis flew overhead, terns screeched, and wrens rasped. As I watched and listened, it felt like a party.

I did not want to forget those Franklin's Gulls, but I've forgotten lots of birds. What makes a bird memorable? It could be the bird itself—perhaps a Pileated Woodpecker at your local park or a sparrow returning to your feeder for yet another year. It could be a bird's behavior—a hummingbird sitting on a nest or a Peregrine stooping. It could also be what we bring to the observation. Showing my grandchildren their first plunging pelican would be memorable to me.

Todd Newberry has suggested that if we can't remember a bird on our list, we need to cross it off. I don't want to cull my list. Maybe my story about being at a bird party will help me remember those gulls. Of course, the birds weren't having a party that morning. I made that up. Why do we bird? To make memories.

Solace

Birding can be a kind of meditation. When I am looking at a bird or listening to it, my thinking mind momentarily disappears and there is just me-and-the-bird. When the bird flies or stops singing I start to think again, but my thoughts disappear when I see or hear another bird.

Sierra Valley is an excellent place to focus the mind. Fifty miles northwest of Reno and roughly sixty square miles, it is ringed by low hills on three sides. The crest of the Sierra Nevada rises sharply to the west. I went there with the hawk-guys one warm, late June day. Songbirds were singing from the trees and bushes, and snipe were standing on fence posts.

The birdiest spot in the valley is an oasis of water and marshes surrounded by drier fields. We got out of the van beyond the last farmhouse. Four Black Terns fluttered above the pond near the road. Bright Wilson's Phalaropes dabbed and swooshed their beaks from side to side as they fed on the water's surface, and a male Ruddy Duck swam by in its psychedelic breeding plumage. Then my arms got tired; I began to think of those lighter binoculars I could have bought. The birding moment was gone.

Meditation instructions often direct us to focus our attention on our breath. When we become aware of our thoughts or emotions (or our binoculars) we are supposed to notice them and then return our attention to our breath. Birders can substitute birds for breath. I look at a meadowlark perched on a close sagebrush, absorbed by its bright yellow breast. The bird flies. I follow its brown back and white-lined tail until it disappears in a distant field. Only then do I wonder what other birds are here. Isn't focusing on an avocet in a nearby pond a way of returning to the meditative state? The bird absorbs all my attention; no thoughts intrude.

Beyond a narrow bridge we stopped our vehicle to look at an American Bittern that was so close to the road's edge even its yellow eyes seemed large. The photographer in our group quietly took its picture as it stood with its beak pointed skyward. No one spoke. Were we silent because we were lost in the moment? The bird stood motionless in its bizarre posture. After a long while we drove slowly forward, the bird flew back into the marsh, and we began to talk again. Where had we gone? I had gone to bittern.

The next morning we visited nearby Yuba Pass. Scattered snow patches still shuttered parts of the mile-high meadow. We heard melodious White-crowned Sparrows and an insistent MacGillivray's Warbler. Each bird added its voice to the chorus. A distant woodpecker and a vocal Mountain Quail were the rhythm section. Then a Hermit Thrush began to sing. I closed my eyes. Here was the local group's featured soloist. Someday I will focus all my attention on a singing Hermit Thrush until I breathe its song.

For fifteen years I took annual bird trips with the hawk-guys. Then Marty, my best friend in the group, in only his sixtieth year suffered dementia. While he still could, we all wanted to take one last trip together.

Our first destination was the Diablo Range, east and south of San Jose. Just a ninety minute drive from where we lived, it still looked like the California of a hundred years ago; the slopes are too steep to develop into foothill ranchettes. Birders usually explore this area in the spring, when the breeding birds are loud and colorful, but I did not think our trip could

Greater Roadrunner

wait that long. Marty already had trouble sharing thoughts and feelings, and his short-term memory was almost gone.

When we told him about the trip he was excited. He still wanted to see birds. John Baker wrote "honest observation is [not] enough. The emotions and behavior of the watcher are also facts, and they must be truthfully recorded."[1] I wanted to go birding with Marty one last time, but I did not know what the trip would reveal.

Early the first morning at a roadside pull-out I estimated an extraordinary two hundred Western Bluebirds and three hundred Cedar Waxwings in the sky, in the tops of trees, and on the fence near our van. Many were feeding on mistletoe berries. Marty seemed to enjoy the big flocks. A few pull-outs later we learned that dementia had not impaired his ability to find birds. He was the one to spot a distant woodpecker half-way up a hill against the side of a burnt tree. Later a Greater Roadrunner ran, paused, and ran again along the base of a cliff. I was glad to show it to him. He had seen roadrunners as a child in Southern California.

At one stop Marty tried to tell us that Native Americans had used buckeye seed pods to paralyze and then catch fish. He was looking at a buckeye tree as he talked but was un-able to remember its name. It took us a while to figure out what he meant. After staring at the depth of his loss and my helplessness to do anything about it, I consoled myself with the thought that birding was a perfect activity for him to-day. Though he could not keep up an extended conversation or always remember the name of what he was looking at, he could still find birds and could still look at the ones we called out. There is much more to birding than the names of birds, and I knew he felt that.

We left the Diablo Range at mid-day and drove south to some of the few remaining marshes in the Central Valley. It

1. John Baker, *The Peregrine* (Moscow, ID, University of Idaho Press, 1967) 14.

was a Saturday in November, a duck-hunting day. We saw more decoys than ducks. We also saw Marty's short-term memory problem when, just after our car flushed a bittern, he asked if we had seen one. A minute later, though, he was the first to point out a distant flight of Snow Geese.

On the last morning before returning home, we visited the Merced Wildlife Refuge. A Short-eared Owl flew from one of the few trees in sight and Mourning Doves cooed. Were the doves making the other hawk-guys feel sadder, too? I asked Marty the next week what he liked best about the trip. "The owl," he said with a grin.

Migratory birds are inspirational. They appear each spring in fresh plumage, the singers in full song, having flown hundreds or thousands of miles, and they remind us it is time to renew ourselves again. The best way to receive their message is to go out to the woods or fields and hear these immaculately robed preachers seem to praise the sun, the new buds, the insect hatches, and the joy of hope. Scott Weidensaul said that "bird migration is the one truly unifying natural phenomenon in the world."[1]

One year in late April, when many Neotropical migrants pass through California on the way to their breeding grounds, Helen, her husband, Paul, and I joined others in an overnight hike through the Sutter Buttes. The buttes are an island of oaks and rocky crags about ten miles across, with six peaks over sixteen hundred feet, in the middle of the low Central Valley. The valley's towns, farms, and freeways were invisible and inaudible as we walked and birded.

---

1. Scott Weidensaul, *Living on the Wind: Across the Hemisphere with Migratory Birds* (New York, North Point Press, 1999) x.

In an open forest of blue oak we put our day packs down and chased a flock of warblers up a hillside. None would nest here. Where were they going? We listened for birdsong as we hiked and reached our campsite in mid-afternoon, just before the pick-up truck arrived with the rest of our gear and a fried chicken dinner. The leader of our group said he had expected to hear more *Empidonax* flycatchers, but birders can never expect all their listing prayers to be answered.

We are all on our own migrations, psychological as well as physical, and Paul was at a difficult crossing. His cancer, which had been in remission, had returned. This was his last camping trip. That night, awake in my sleeping bag, I remembered some of the birding trips we had taken together over the past fifteen years: the time he found a Great Horned Owl perched in a distant tree one afternoon; how he liked to bet a quarter on the number of species we would see each day; how he was always eager to look for one more bird.

The next morning, before resuming our hike, a few of us climbed one of the nearby buttes. Paul went to the top. He always liked to stand on the summit and look into the distance. The rest of us stayed lower and looked for birds. Maybe he was looking for something else.

We hiked out of the buttes at mid-day through green spring fields that had not yet turned brown in the soon-to-arrive summer heat. If only we could turn around and walk back to the campsite, have someone bring us chicken dinner every night, have this spring never end and Paul get well. I looked at him. He was looking at a meadowlark.

Paul died that October. In early November I asked Helen if she wanted to go birding the day after Thanksgiving. The three of us had often taken a bird trip on that weekend, and I thought she might like to look for birds between her waves of grief. She said yes, she wanted to come.

As we ascended the south fork of the Yuba River, the birds were few and the sky was overcast. In the quiet that filled the car I wondered if the trip was a mistake. When we descended Yuba Pass, a Northern Goshawk swiped across the road. Helen was looking inward and did not see it.

In Sierra Valley the sky was still overcast and the wind made us put on extra clothing. We did get a close look at a Ferruginous Hawk on a pole, but birds were still scarce. We drove back to the interstate on an unpaved road through a silent forest. At a reservoir, when we looked through our scopes, a distant flock of ducks became Canvasbacks and goldeneyes. One of the shapes proved to be a Common Loon. By now Helen was looking outward again and seeing birds. Then the temperature really began to fall and she got cold. We drove home. Months later Helen twice thanked me for taking her birding that day. She said it helped her keep going and gave her something to do besides be sad.

Three years after Paul died, on the day after Thanksgiving, Helen and I birded the Nature Conservancy's Cosumnes River Preserve in the Central Valley. She had spent the holiday itself with family. It was foggy when we met at the Preserve, and the birds were not active. Though the early birder does see more birds, we could have waited another hour. Soon another car arrived. Two men in their forties, with binoculars around their necks, got out. They were there, they said, to see "whatever birds we can" and hiked off down the trail.

When the fog lifted we birded some nearby ponds. Four more cars were parked by the roadside and four more groups of birders were looking at the ducks and geese. By mid-afternoon twelve more cars had brought two dozen birders to look at the ducks and geese and, by now, even some shorebirds at the ponds. Small flocks of cranes called as they flew overhead.

A man with a white beard was talking to some college students. Some people were consulting field guides and then looking again through their scopes. It was like a party: birders and their birds.

I propose we designate the Friday after Thanksgiving as National Birding Day. Since it gets dark early, we could bird and still get home for a dinner of the feast's leftovers. The weekend still lies ahead. National Birding Day would celebrate not how many birds we see, but what birds have to offer us. That night, we could give thanks a second time.

Six years later Helen developed chronic bronchitis. While she waited for western and eastern medicine to clear her lungs, I wanted to see if some bird medicine might also help, so I suggested a Berkeley Big Year, or BBY as we came to call it: how many birds could we find in one year in the city where we lived. Now she had another reason to look for birds in her backyard.

She liked the idea. We asked two other local birders, Emilie and Kay, to join us and we all agreed the BBY would not be a competition. If we found a new bird, we would phone or email each other to report its location. The only rule was that the bird had to be within the city limits.

Kay assumed the role of list keeper and cartographer. The vinyl-protected map she made for us was particularly important because just east of Berkeley is a large regional park with many resident, wintering, and breeding birds—all outside the city limit. Sometimes a bird crossed the city line—thank you, House Wren; sometimes the bird didn't—come closer, Swainson's Thrush.

Remember treasure hunts? It was fun to find that red sock or smooth rock. The BBY was like that: an Olive-sided

Flycatcher behind the football stadium in July, a Cackling Goose with a flock of Canada Geese near the waterfront in December. Kay did the most treasure hunting. The Ross's Goose she found on December 29 was a vagrant! Emilie found the "power birch tree" in the park across the street from her house that captured Yellow Warblers in September.

In April we did a Berkeley Big Day. Helen was able to join us for a few hours but, unfortunately, left before a man told us he had seen Black-headed Grosbeaks the day before in a small park farther up the hill. We weren't the only people keeping track of the birds in Berkeley; at the park we heard a grosbeak singing. Fortunately, Helen did see the colorful shorebird flock feeding on a mudflat earlier that morning. She would not have seen them without our BBY, even though the birds were only a ten-minute drive from her house.

Daily activities gained an extra dimension for all of us. Emilie added Violet-Green Swallow to our list while eating lunch at an outdoor café. I saw a Cooper's Hawk while walking the dog. An unanticipated delight of the BBY was exploring parts of the city I rarely visited. In September Kay found a southbound MacGillivray's Warbler in a small migrant trap near San Francisco Bay. I didn't know we had a migrant trap in Berkeley.

Helen was better at the end of the year than she was in early January. I can't say the BBY helped her recovery, but I can't say it didn't help either. On December 31 we birded the waterfront for a few hours and added Barrow's Goldeneye—at last. Our final group total was 173 species. According to Kay, we missed ten birds that others had reported during the year. The Black-chinned Hummingbird at Robin's house didn't count. She found it in Berkeley, but it was in a cage when I saw it.

In December, Kay told a friend about our BBY, and he decided to try and organize a friendly big year competition between birders in Arcata and Eureka for the following year. Why not? Every city has bird treasures, and birders are often looking for another reason to bird. Besides, a city big year does not require as much driving as a county or state big year, and you can work on your list by taking a detour on the way to the hardware store.

Helen added European Starling on the last day of the year and ended up with 136 species. Maybe the BBY did help her get better.

A flock of us gathered at the third Mono Basin Bird Chautauqua one summer solstice weekend. David Winkler, an ornithologist and one of the early researchers of Mono Lake's bird life, spoke at the Friday evening dinner. He said there were circles of seasons, circles of friends who learn from each other and from birds, and circles of life. We ourselves are arcs within those circles, as are all the other creatures we share this world with awhile. Yes, and when we die our substance becomes parts of other arcs—not "dust to dust" but "life to life."

Mono Lake inspires this kind of musing. It has the second largest rookery of California Gulls in North America (some 45,000 to 65,000 birds) and nourishes a million and a half Eared Grebes that stop to feed and rest there during their fall migration. It was almost destroyed by Los Angeles' insatiable water diversions, until an environmental protest movement saved the lake for the birds who use it and the people who enjoy it.

Later that evening we listened to Kenn Kaufman talk about how, when he was young in the early 1970s, he hitchhiked two hundred thousand miles around North America in search of birds. When he reached California he went on a pelagic trip with Rich Stallcup. As the waves rolled the boat, Kenn said he was hoping his target birds would show up soon because he was more than ready to return to the dock. Then

Western Tanager

he heard Rich say joyfully that the birders on the boat and the birds on the water were both experiencing the same rough ocean. Kenn said the trip reminded him that birding could be about really watching what the birds were doing as well as identifying them. I have also heard Rich talk about what the world must look like from the bird's point of view while the boat was rocking and I was trying to look at the bird. At the end of Kenn's talk I vowed to be a more complete observer.

The next morning, on a guided bird walk, we watched swallows entering nest boxes and wood-pewees flycatching. I could easily have seen these birds on my own, but I enjoyed being part of the birders' flock. I asked the leader questions about his scope and pointed out a Black-headed Grosbeak to some other birders. I smiled when one man praised the splash of red, black, and yellow of his first male Western Tanager, and I recalled how a tanager with those same colors, across a mountain creek more than thirty years ago, had initiated me to birding.

Most of the dozen people in our group had identified themselves earlier as beginning birders. Their enthusiasm at seeing nesting swallows through a scope made me look longer at birds I might otherwise have only glanced at. I tried to imagine how those swallows saw their world. Except for a bear's slash mark on one aspen's trunk, and the splintered nest box on the ground below, I guessed the swallows were content. They had plenty of insects to eat, a nearby stream for water, and long days to feed their chicks. Who could ask for more?

On the way to my campsite that night I saw the red eye-shine of a Common Poorwill. At dawn a Great Horned Owl perched briefly in the only tree in sight and two Common Nighthawks swooped and *peented* overhead. On the drive home I was giddy with all the weekend's birds.

Our language is rich with the names of flocks: coveys of quail, gaggles of geese, rafts of ducks. To commemorate Mono Lake's continued existence, let's add a squadron of gulls, an invasion of grebes, and a persistence of birders to the dictionary. Since flocks of birders are a common sight at bird festivals, let's also add a stare of binoculars and a scrutiny of scopes.

Maybe birds and birders are part of a larger flock. Maybe, together, we can call ourselves a celebration.

The National Audubon Society's Christmas Bird Count (CBC), during which birders count the number of individual birds of each species in a specified area, is not just about counting birds and providing information about wintering bird populations. CBCs are also an annual, continent-wide opportunity for birders to identify themselves to each other and to nonbirders.

The Oakland CBC always occurs on a Sunday close to the winter solstice. When the tide is high, I ride in a canoe with some of the hawk-guys and keep track of the names and numbers of the water birds in San Leandro Bay. We enter the channels that curve through Arrowhead Marsh and look for rails. The only sound is the rustle of the canoe brushing against the pickleweed. When we flush a Clapper Rail from a small patch of marsh grass that the water has not yet covered, the bird swims awkwardly to a larger patch and tries to hide. A Northern Harrier searches for what prey the high tide might reveal.

If I ignore the Oakland city skyline, it is easy to pretend that the pre-Euro-American past is around the next bend and I will soon see "flocks of geese, ducks, and seabirds ... so enormous that when alarmed by a rifle shot they were said to rise 'in a dense cloud with a noise like that of a hurricane.'"[1] Then the noise of a plane from the Oakland Airport reminds me the marsh is now irrevocably an urban wildlife refuge.

CBCs encourage newcomers to participate. Helen said that many years ago, after she and her twelve-year-old son (now an ornithologist) had participated in their first CBC, they went to the evening dinner and were amazed to learn that some one hundred and seventy species had been seen that day less than ten miles from their house. They had seen some of those species only in their field guide and added a few to their life lists the next day.

By late December I am mildly edgy, eager for more light and even for the start of spring migration. The Oakland CBC is one way I celebrate the end of the year and the beginning of the next. San Keen wrote that birders, "... practitioners of a natural theology ... [are] blessed with ... the capacity to see ... the presence of the sacred in the precision flying of a flock ..."[2] I agree. After thirty years of counting the birds on a Sunday in December, rain and shine, I have come to count on them: our seasons are now intertwined.

1. Malcolm Margolin, *The Ohlone Way* (Berkeley, CA, Heyday Books, 1978) 7.
2. Sam Keen, *Sightings: Extraordinary Encounters with Ordinary Birds* (San Francisco, CA, Chronicle Books, 2007) 112, 118.

One of the most fascinating things about [birding] is its delightful uncertainty; you never know what's in store for you as you start out; you never can tell what will happen next ... "

Notes

Introduction

Other authors also describe birding as a kind of attraction. Tim Dee tries to see birds "as if for the first time but with eyes informed by years of seeing, to capture life looking at life."[1] Luke Dempsey described his first Common Yellowthroat this way: "There—that's the sound of love as it begins."[2] Richard Cannings wrote, "Whatever the origins of … [my] interest [in birds], it is indeed an enchantment."[3]

Lawrence Kilham said, after watching a pair of Sandhill Cranes for several months, "I loved the birds, and it was thrilling to enter into their lives as much as I did. Quiet watching: what a feeling of the immensity and wonder of nature it can give you!"[4]

Joseph Kastner wrote "it is hard … not to believe that watching birds generally involves a kind of love."[5] Simon Barnes looks at birds "… because looking at birds is one of life's greatest pleasures and looking at birds is a key: it opens doors, and if you choose to go through them you find you enjoy life more and understand life better."[6]

1. Tim Dee, *The Running Sky* (London, Jonathan Cape, 2009) 4.

2. Luke Dempsey, *A Supremely Bad Idea: Three Mad Birders and Their Quest to See It All* (New York, Bloomsbury, 2008) 11.

3. Richard Cannings, *An Enchantment of Birds* (Vancouver, Canada, Greystone Books, 2007) viii.

4. Lawrence Kilham, *On Watching Birds* (Chelsea, VT, Chelsea Green Publishing Company) 98.

5. Joseph Kastner, *A World of Watchers* (San Francisco, CA, Sierra Club Books, 1986) 5.

6. Simon Barnes, *How To Be a Bad Birdwatcher* (New York, Pantheon Books, 2005) 4.

Flight, Song, Color

Simon Barnes said "there are many good reasons for becoming a birdlistener ... but the greatest of all reasons ... is that each and every bird is capable of making the listener happy: for an instant, for a day, for a season, for a lifetime."[1]

Surprises

Birds can surprise us in many ways. Elliott Coues wrote, "For myself, the time is past, happily or not, when every bird was an agreeable surprise, for dewdrops do not last all day; but ... one bird new to a locality would repay a week's search ..."[2] One hundred years later, Chuck Bernstein echoed him: "For me every birdwalk is an adventure, imbued with romance ... No matter how parochial the area or how commonplace the birds, there is always some new excitement, always something to be learned in watching carefully."[3] Jen Hill said "Birds offer us an opportunity to be surprised and affirmed, to know that there exist some things that exceed us ..."[4]

Conservation

John Fitzpatrick said in 2004 that the long term goal was to "ensure [the] persistence of all American bird populations in their natural numbers, natural habitats, and natural geographical ranges ..."[5] We have a long way to go.

---

1. Simon Barnes, *Bird Watching with Your Eyes Closed* (London, Short Books, 2012) 249-250.

2. Elliott Coues, *Key to North American Birds, Vol 1* (New York, Arno Press, 1974) 11.

3. Chuck Bernstein, *The Joy of Birding* (Santa Barbara, CA, Capra Press, 1984) 15-16.

4. Jen Hill, *An Exhilaration of Wings* (New York, Viking, 1999) xviii.

5. Edward S. Brinkley and Paul J. Baicich, "The Changing Seasons: Rome Burning?" (*North American Birds*, American Birding Association, 2004) 477.

Solace

Julie Zickefoose, who has rehabilitated injured birds for many years, wrote "I live for the moment when my gaze meets a bird's—that exchange of awareness of the 'who' in each of us, the spark of understanding leaping from the bright bead of its eye to mine."[1]

John Hay wrote, "Birds fly away from us, with an unspoken invitation to follow after."[2] Sy Montgomery said birds "always come into my life at critical moments to enrich my spirit and enlarge my heart."[3]

1. Julie Zickefoose, "The Bluebird Effect: Uncommon Bonds with Common Birds" (New York, Houghton Mifflin Harcourt Publishing Company, 2012) 36–37.

2. John Hay, *The Great House of Birds* (San Francisco, CA, Sierra Club Books, 1996) xii.

3. Sy Montgomery, *Birdology* (New York, Free Press, 2010) 1.

One day's exposure to mountains is better than carloads of books."

 John Muir

References

Baker, John. *The Peregrine.* Moscow, ID, University of Idaho Press, 1967.

Baptista, Luis Felipe. *Song Dialects and Demes in Sedentary Populations of the White-Crowned Sparrow.* Berkeley, CA, University of California Press, 1975.

Barnes, Simon. *How To Be a Bad Birdwatcher.* New York, Pantheon Books, 2005.

Barnes, Simon. *Bird Watching with Your Eyes Closed.* London, UK, Short Books, 2012.

Bernstein, Chuck. *The Joy of Birding.* Santa Barbara, CA, Capra Press, 1984.

Brewer, William H. *Up and Down California in 1860–1864.* Berkeley, CA, University of California Press, 1974.

Brinkley, Edward S. and Baicich, Paul J. "The Changing Seasons: Rome Burning?" *North American Birds*, Volume 58: No. 4, 2004, p. 474–485.

Cannings, Richard. *An Enchantment of Birds.* Vancouver, Canada, Greystone Books, 2007.

Cashwell, Peter. *The Verb 'To Bird': Sightings of an Avid Birder.* Philadelphia, PA, Paul Dry Books, 2003.

Cocker, Mark. *Birders: Tales of a Tribe.* New York, Atlantic Monthly Press, 2001.

Coues, Elliott. *Key to North American Birds, Volume 1.* New York, Arno Press, 1974.

Dawson, William Leon. *The Birds of California, Volume 2,3.* San Diego, CA, South Moulton Company, 1923.

Dee, Tim. *The Running Sky: A Birdwatching Life.* London, Jonathan Cape, 2009.

Dempsey, Luke. *A Supremely Bad Idea: Three Mad Birders and Their Quest to See It All.* New York, Bloomsbury, 2008.

Dunne, Pete. *The Feather Quest: A North American Birder's Year.* New York, Peregrine Books USA, Inc., 1992.

Haupt, Lyanda Lynn. *Rare Encounters with Ordinary Birds.* Seattle, WA, Sasquatch Books, 2001.

Hay, John (ed.). *The Great House of Birds: Classic Writings About Birds.* San Francisco, CA, Sierra Club Books, 1996.

Hill, Jennifer (ed.). *An Exhilaration of Wings: The Literature of Birdwatching.* New York, Viking, 1999.

Howell, Steven N. G. "Letters to the Editor." *Birding,* Vol. 36: No. 5, 2004, p. 457–458.

Kastner, Joseph. *A World of Watchers.* San Francisco, CA, Sierra Club Books, 1986.

Kaufman, Kenn. *Kingbird Highway.* Boston, MA, Houghton Mifflin Company, 1997.

Kaufman, Kenn. *Flights Against the Sunset.* Boston, MA, Houghton Mifflin Company, 2008.

Keen, Sam. *Sightings: Extraordinary Encounters with Ordinary Birds.* San Francisco, CA, Chronicle Books, 2007.

Kilham, Lawrence. *On Watching Birds.* Chelsea, VT, Chelsea Green Publishing Company, 1988.

Koeppel, Dan. *To See Every Bird on Earth: A Father, a Son, and a Lifelong Obsession.* New York, A Plume Book, Penguin Group, 2006.

Kroodsma, Donald. *The Singing Life of Birds: The Art and Science of Listening to Birdsong.* Boston, MA, Houghton Mifflin Company, 2005.

Leopold, Aldo. *A Sand County Almanac.* New York, Ballantine Books, 1974.

Levine, George. *Lifebirds.* New Brunswick, NJ, Rutgers University Press, 1995.

Margolin, Malcolm. *The Ohlone Way*. Berkeley, CA, Heyday Books, 1978.

Matthiessen, Peter. *The Birds of Heaven: Travels with Cranes*. New York, North Point Press, 2001.

Montgomery, Sy. *Birdology*. New York, Free Press, 2010.

Mynott, Jeremy. *Birdscapes: Birds in Our Imagination and Experience*. Princeton, NJ, Princeton University Press, 2009.

Nathan, Leonard. *Diary of a Left-Handed Birdwatcher*. San Diego, CA, Harcourt Brace and Company, 1996.

Newberry, Todd and Holtan, Gene. *The Ardent Birder*. Berkeley, CA, Ten Speed Press, 2005.

North American Bird Conservation Initiative in the United States. U.S. NABCI Committee, Executive Summary, September 2000. A Vision of American Bird Conservation. U.S. Fish and Wildlife Service, Washington, DC. http://digitalmedia.fws.gov/cdm/ref/collection/document/id/1443

North American Bird Conservation Initiative. U.S. Committee, 2009. The State of the Birds, United States of America, 2009. U.S. Department of Interior: Washington, DC. www.stateofthebirds.org

Obmascik, Mark. *The Big Year: A Tale of Man, Nature, and Fowl Obsession*. New York, Free Press, 2004.

Rosen, Jonathan. *The Life of the Skies*. New York, Farrar, Straus and Giroux, 2008.

Sibley, David Allen. *Sibley's Birding Basics*. New York, Alfred A. Knopf, 2002.

Skutch, Alexander Frank. *The Minds of Birds*. College Station, TX, Texas A and M Press, 1996.

Stallcup, Rich. *Ocean Birds of the Nearshore Pacific*. Stinson Beach, CA, Point Reyes Bird Observatory, 1990.

Stallcup, Rich. "Listing for Life." Observer, Quarterly Journal of the Point Reyes Bird Observatory, Number 120, Spring, 2000, p. 9.

Taylor, Rick. "On Listing." *Birding*, Vol. 36: No. 1, 2004, p. 50–51.

Weidensaul, Scott. *Living on the Wind*. New York, North Point Press, 1999.

Wright, Rick. "Discovery." *Winging It*, Vol. 18, No. 1, 2006, p. 2.

Zickefoose, Julie. *The Bluebird Effect: Uncommon Bonds with Common Birds*. New York, Houghton Mifflin Harcourt Publishing Company, 2012.

I would venture that birding ... is at base an emotional enterprise. ... What sustains us are intense attachments to nature, nourished by our encounters. Those of us who feel these stirrings of the heart really are what the epithet calls us: ardent birders.

🖎 Todd Newberry

Acknowledgments

I have shared many birding adventures with friends over the past forty years. Although birding alone can be enjoyable, seeing the bird with someone else provides a deeper pleasure for me. Thank you, all. I would particularly like to thank the friends who appear in this book by first name only: Helen Green, the late Paul Green, Kay Loughman, Frank Lowe, Robin Pulich, Emilie Strauss, Janet Stock, and the hawk guys: Fred Conrad, Steve Monrad, the late Marty Reutinger, and the late Elliott Smith.

I am also grateful to everyone who took time to read earlier versions of the manuscript. Many friends, friends of friends, family members, and acquaintances offered encouragement and helpful suggestions, including Amanda Abarbanel-Rice, Alan Berne, Chuck Brickley, Helen Davie, Cherie Hunter Day, Ken Green, Tracy Koretsky, Lynne Leach, Bob Lewis, Jennie McDonald, the late Ira Polonsky, Barbara Rice, Jeanne Rice, Phila Rogers, and Ebba Story. It took ten years to complete this book and, if I have left some readers out, I apologize.

Todd Newberry, author of *The Ardent Birder* (Ten Speed Press), read an earlier version of the manuscript and told me I needed to re-organize the text. Without his help, *Why We Bird* would still be a collection of unconnected bird stories. He then volunteered to line-edit the revised manuscript. I cannot thank him enough.

Robin Pulich graciously agreed to illustrate the manuscript. I very much appreciate her willingness to take on this project. Her delightful pictures brighten the text!

Without Helen Green, this book might not exist at all. I have used the stories of our trips up-and-down California, and the trips I took with her and her late husband, Paul, to describe many of the reasons why we bird. Many, many thanks for all those California field days.

Ellis Myers cheerfully designed the book. Thank you!

Finally, I would like to thank my wife, Carol Shattuck-Rice, not a birder, who knows a lot more about birds than all her friends, for her continual enthusiasm and support.

Parts of *Why We Bird* have been previously published in a slightly different form: the misidentification incident was a letter to the editor of *Birding*, Vol. 34: No. 1, 2002, p. 11–12; the Mono Lake Chautauqua vignette appeared in the May/June 2009 issue of *Bird Watcher's Digest*, p. 58–61 as "The Mono Basin Bird Chautauqua"; the bird banding section is posted on the San Francisco Bay Bird Observatory's *Field Log*, www.sfbbo.org/volunteer/fieldlog; and the story about taking one last hawk-guy trip appeared in *Birding*, Vol. 44, No. 4. 2012, p. 68–69 as "I Will Remember That Owl."

*W*hat I like about [bird]-watching ... is that it not only strengthens my bonds with the beauty of nature, but also my empathy with living things."

 Lawrence Kilham

Biographical Notes

David Rice has a junior member National Audubon Society pin on his bulletin board but did not start actively birding until his mid-twenties. He lives in Berkeley, California with his wife and works as a clinical psychologist. Three children and three grandchildren also live in the Bay Area. He is a co-author of the *Alameda County Breeding Bird Atlas*.

Robin Pulich is an artist, writer, attorney, wildlife rehabilitator, and old rose gardener. She resides in Berkeley, California with her husband, Frank. Her favorite pastimes of hiking, camping, and birdwatching shape the focus of her art. For over twenty years she has cared for injured and orphaned hummingbirds, poorwills, and small songbirds such as kinglets and warblers in her home and backyard aviary as a volunteer for the Lindsay Wildlife Museum.